Vegetarian Dessert Recipes- Kid Friendly Sweets and Treats

Vegetarian Cookbook Cooking Series

© Copyright
All Rights Reserved, Madson

@ www.kids-cooking-activities.com

All rights Reserved. No part of this publication or the information in it may be quoted from or reproduced in any form by means such as printing, scanning, photocopying or otherwise without prior written permission of the copyright holder.

Disclaimer and Terms of Use: Effort has been made to ensure that the information in this book is accurate and complete, however, the author and the publisher do not warrant the accuracy of the information, text and graphics contained within the book due to the rapidly changing nature of science, research, known and unknown facts and internet. The Author and the publisher do not hold any responsibility for errors, omissions, or contrary interpretation of the subject matter herein. This book is presented solely for motivational and informational purposes only.

Table of Contents

Desserts 4
   Chocolate Chip Cookie Dip 4
   Monkey Bites 5
   Vegan Chocolate Cake 6
   Butterscotch Brownies 7
   5 Ingredient Pumpkin Dessert 8
   Mini Homemade Peppermint Patties 9
   Protein Bites 11
   Vegan Cake Balls 12
   Raw Almond Butter Cups 14
   No Bake Chocolate Macaroons 15
   2 Ingredient Frosting 16
   Maple Cookies 17
   Almond Joy Cookies 18
   Chocolate Cereal Bars 20
   Sweet Cinnamon Sticky Buns 21
   Monkey's Chocolate Chip Donuts 22
   Carrot Cake Balls 23
   Pumpkin Spice Dip 24
   Chocolate Orange Avocado Pudding 25
   Chocolate Mousse 26
   Vegan Lemon Meltaways 27
   Vegan Twinkie Cake 28

Vanilla Cake 29
Sugar and Cinnamon Chips 30
Vegan Jell-O 31
Spiced Almond Milk 32
Vegan Orange Julius 33
Vegan Banana Pops 34
Vanilla Avocado Banana "Ice Cream" 35
Banana Bread Biscotti 36

Desserts

Chocolate Chip Cookie Dip
Ingredients
About one half-pound of yellow potatoes-make sure they're peeled & cooked (comes out to about 1 &1/3 Cup mashed potatoes
6-7 T. Organic maple syrup to taste
4 TBSP cashew butter
1 TBSP vanilla extract
Sea salt to taste
1/4 Cup of vegan chocolate chips

Directions:
In your blender or food processor, add the still warm cooked potatoes, cashew butter, maple syrup and vanilla. Cold potatoes are not preferred as warm potatoes create a better texture, silkier and more elegant.
Blend until creamy for several minutes. You should be stopping at times to scrape down your ingredients for an evenly blended mixture. Make sure you're clump free! You will want your batter to be a lovely silky texture. You control how sweet you want your dip by adding a little more or little less maple syrup.
Don't forget to salt to your liking as well!
Place your batter in the refrigerator for approximately 30 minutes to chill. Next you or your child can stir in the chocolate chips-I find dark chocolate work best.

Serve dip with vegan and/or gluten-free cookies or graham crackers, fresh fruit, sugared bagel, or pita chips, or with just a spoon.

Monkey Bites

Here's a quick, animal product free, frozen treat. This recipe requires only four ingredients and is fun and healthy too!

Ingredients
2 large organic bananas
1/8 Cup almond butter
1/8 Cup applesauce
1 Cup chocolate chips

Directions:
Peel two bananas, then slice into 1/4" pieces. Mix the almond butter with the organic applesauce in a small bowl. Spread the mixture onto one of the banana slices and stack on top of a second banana slice making a sandwich. Then put the banana sandwiches on a flat surface that has been lined with freezer paper and put in your freezer for about 20 minutes. Before you remove the bananas from out of your freezer, melt 1 cup of dark chocolate chips. Remove your frozen banana sandwiches from your freezer and drizzle the chocolate over or dip them into the chocolate. Once you've dipped or drizzled over all your bananas, put banana sandwiches in the freezer until chocolate hardens.

~This is such an excellent treat for adults, and children alike, at about 30 calories each.

Vegan Chocolate Cake
Ingredients
1 1/2 Cups sugar
2 tsp vanilla
1/4 Cup coconut oil or vegetable oil
1/4 Cup applesauce
1 1/2 Cups water
1 1/2 tsp vinegar
1/2 Cup cocoa
1 1/2 tsp baking soda
2 Cups flour
1 tsp salt

Directions
In a mixer, blend together sugar, vanilla, oil, applesauce, water, and vinegar. Add cocoa, baking soda, flour and salt and blend together until well combined. Pour into a greased 13x9 pan and bake at 350 degrees for 20-25 minutes or until toothpick inserted in middle comes out clean.

Butterscotch Brownies

Recipes for butterscotch brownies are as old as the hills, but this delightful recipe nails it each time. This recipe for vegan butterscotch brownies is awesome for busy moms and a sweets-craving.

Ingredients
1 Cup vegan margarine
1 1/2 Cup brown sugar
1 1/2 Cup wheat flour
1 T. baking powder
1/4 tsp salt
1 T. vanilla extract
1 Cup ground flax seed mixed with 1/3 Cup soy milk (you can substitute almond or hemp milk for the soy milk if desired)
1/4 Cup chopped walnuts
1/2 Cup organic unsweetened, medium shredded coconut

Directions:
Preheat oven to 350 degrees. Grease a 9" x 9" baking pan. Whip flax seed and soy milk mixture, or you could use an egg substitute here. Incorporate your baking powder, flour, and salt. Melt the vegetable margarine. Remove the batter from heat and mix in your vanilla and brown sugar. Next, stir in the walnuts, shredded coconut, or even chocolate chips Mix in your dry ingredients at this point.

Pour evenly into greased pan and bake for approximately 25 minutes. Voilà! You've made a tasty treat you can be proud to feed your family, in practically no time at all.

5 Ingredient Pumpkin Dessert

It doesn't have to be Halloween to fall in love with pumpkin.

Ingredients
1 lb. silken tofu
2/3 Cup organic maple syrup
1 Cup cooked pumpkin, unsweetened
1/2 tsp cinnamon
1/4 tsp cloves
dash of salt

Directions:
In a blender, add tofu, maple syrup, pumpkin, salt, and spices. Blend until creamy and smooth. Let chill in freezer.

Mini Homemade Peppermint Patties

A favorite store-bought candy made right in your home. These sneak into the movies just as easily as the national brand too!

Ingredients
1/2 Cup cashews
1/2 Cup coconut oil
3 T. agave nectar
2 T. almond or coconut milk
1 tsp peppermint extract
3/4 Cup dark chocolate chips
1/2 T. coconut oil

Directions:
Add the cashews, 1/2 cup of melted coconut oil, agave to taste, almond or coconut milk, and peppermint extract into a high-speed blender or food processor. Blend on the highest speed until completely smooth. Line a baking sheet with parchment paper and ready mini candy liners. Add a half tablespoon of filling into each liner. Place on the baking sheet. Freeze, uncovered, for 20 minutes or until firm. After freezing, quickly pop the patties out of the cupcake liners and set each on top of their respective liner. Return to the freezer for 10 minutes to firm up even more.

In the meantime, melt the chocolate and coconut oil in a small pot over the lowest heat. When half of the chips have melted, remove it from heat and stir until chips are melted. Allow the chocolate to cool slightly before dunking the patties. Remove the patties from the freezer and dunk them into the melted chocolate with a fork. Tap the side to shake off excess chocolate and place on parchment paper. Do this step as quickly as possible so the patties won't melt. Return the patties to your freezer for about 10 minutes. Enjoy!

Protein Bites
Ingredients
1 Cup Medjool dates
1/4 Cup hulled hemp seed
1/4 Cup Chia seed
1/4 Cup sesame seed
1/4 Cup natural cocoa powder
1/2 tsp vanilla extract
1/4 tsp cinnamon
1/4 tsp fine salt or less, according to taste
1/4 Cup raw cacao nibs (or mini dark chocolate chips)

Directions:
Add your pitted dates into blender or food processor and process until a chunky paste forms. Add the hemp seed, chia seed, sesame seed, natural cocoa powder, pure vanilla extract, cinnamon, and salt. Process until thoroughly mixed.

Add in the dark chocolate chips or cacao nibs. The dough should be sticky when pressed. If it's not sticky enough to shape into balls, add a small amount of water and
process until it comes together. Form into balls.

Vegan Cake Balls
Ingredients for the cake
1 Cup coconut milk
1 T. organic apple cider vinegar
1/3 Cup. grapeseed oil
1/2 T. vanilla extract
1 Cup organic coconut or cane sugar
1 1/2 Cups gluten-free all-purpose flour
1/3 Cup sifted cocoa powder
1 tsp baking soda
3/4 tsp fine sea salt

Ingredients for the cake frosting
1 can full-fat chilled coconut milk
4 oz non-dairy semi-sweet chocolate chips or dark chocolate
1 tsp coconut oil

Toppings:
shredded coconut, mashed candy canes, chopped nuts, sprinkles, etc.

Directions:
Chill a can of coconut milk overnight. Preheat oven to 350 degrees F and grease a muffin tin. In a large bowl, stir the milk with the apple cider vinegar. Let it sit for a few minutes to curdle, making vegan buttermilk. With an electric beater or mixer, beat in the grapeseed oil, cane or coconut sugar, and pure vanilla, into the almond milk mixture. Add dry ingredients. Beat until smooth. Evenly distribute the batter among cupcake liners. I like to use an ice cream scoop with a spring release button. Bake cake at 350F for approx. 20 minutes. Cool cupcakes. Crumble cake into a large bowl. Scoop out coconut cream from the can. Add just a little bit of cream at a

time to the crumbled cake, being mindful to not over saturate the cake. Shape cake dough into 1" diameter balls and freeze the balls for 30 minutes, or until firm. Melt chocolate and coconut oil in a saucepan over low heat. When 2/3 of the chips are melted, remove from heat source, and stir until chips are melted. Dip the balls into the chocolate and swirl until fully coated. Tip off excess and move to a cooling rack with paper towels underneath so the chocolate can drip off. Sprinkle with chopped nuts, broken peppermint candies, coconut, or sprinkles. Transfer to fridge to set chocolate
for a few minutes, then enjoy!!

Raw Almond Butter Cups
Ingredients for the base
3/4 Cup raw almonds, ground into a meal
1/4 Cup certified gluten-free rolled oats, ground into a flour
2 T. raw almond butter
1 1/2 T. coconut oil
1 1/2 T. agave nectar or pure maple syrup
1/4 tsp cinnamon
1/4 tsp vanilla extract
A pinch of fine grain salt, to taste

Ingredients for the topping
3 T. coconut oil
3 T. pure maple syrup
2 T. cocoa powder
pinch of fine grain sea salt, to taste

Directions:
Add 3/4 of a cup of almonds and organic oats into a high-speed blender, mixer, or food processor. Blend on high until a flour type mixture forms. Transfer to a large bowl and break up any clumps with fingers. Add the almond nut butter, coconut oil, agave or maple syrup, vanilla, cinnamon, vanilla, and salt into the bowl. Stir until thoroughly incorporated. The dough should be the consistency of cookie dough now. Line a mini muffin tin with liners. Portion the dough into each muffin cup and press until smooth.

To make your chocolate sauce, whisk together the cocoa powder, sweetener, salt, and coconut oil until no clumps are seen. Drizzle the sauce over top each of the cups with a spoon. Garnish cups with sliced almonds if you would like. Place in your freezer for 30 minutes or until firm. Pop out the cups and enjoy cold!

No Bake Chocolate Macaroons
Ingredients
1 banana mashed
1/4 Cup coconut oil
1/4 Cup pure maple syrup
1/2 tsp vanilla extract
6 T. sifted cocoa powder
1 1/2 Cup unsweetened shredded coconut
1 T. chia seeds
small pinch of fine grain sea salt, to taste

Directions:
In a medium mixing bowl, mash banana until almost all the clumps are gone. Stir in the melted coconut oil, vanilla, and maple syrup. Sift in the cocoa powder and stir until combined. Now stir in the coconut, optional chia seeds, and fine grain sea salt to taste. Line a baking sheet with parchment paper. Using a spoon or ice cream scooper, scoop balls onto the sheet. Place sheet in the freezer for around 20 minutes, or until macaroons are firm. Enjoy!

2 Ingredient Frosting
Ingredients
1 can full-fat coconut milk
1 bag dark, non-dairy chocolate chips

Directions
Chill a can of full-fat coconut milk in the fridge overnight. When ready, flip can over and open with can opener. Pour off the water. Scoop only the solid white coconut cream into a pot. Add the chocolate chips into the pot as well and gently melt the coconut cream and the chocolate chips together over low heat. Stirring frequently and be careful not to burn. Transfer the mixture into a bowl and then into the fridge until it firms up enough to whip into frosting. When it's firmed enough to your liking, whip it with beaters until smooth. If it's still too firm, you can leave it out on the counter a bit longer.

Maple Cookies
Ingredients
1 Cup vegan butter
3/4 Cup granulated sugar
3/4 Cup brown sugar
1/2 Cup maple syrup
1/2 Cup vanilla non-dairy yogurt
2 Cups all-purpose flour
1 Cup wheat flour
1 tsp cinnamon
1 tsp baking powder
1/2 tsp baking soda
1/2 tsp kosher salt

Directions:
Preheat oven to 350 degrees F. Using electric mixer, cream vegan butter with granulated and brown sugars until fluffed. Beat in the maple syrup and vanilla non-dairy yogurt, until well incorporated. In a separate bowl, whisk together the remaining ingredients. Add dry ingredients to wet ingredients and mix until smooth texture. Scoop the dough by ice cream scooper and place 2" apart on a parchment lined cookie sheet. Bake about 9 minutes, or until lightly browned. Cool on cookie sheet for a couple minutes, then move to a wire rack. Completely cool and enjoy!

Almond Joy Cookies

Your favorite candy, now in cookie form!

Ingredients
1/2 Cup coconut oil
1/2 Cup almond butter
1 Cup brown sugar, packed
1 T. ground flax seeds
1 T. corn starch
3 T. dairy-free milk
1/2 Cup water
1 tsp pure vanilla extract
1 tsp coconut extract
1 1/4 Cup all-purpose flour
3 Cups old fashioned or instant oatmeal
1/2 Cup Hershey's extra dark cocoa
1 tsp baking soda
1 tsp baking powder
1/2 tsp sea salt
1 Cup coconut flakes
1 Cup dairy-free semi-sweet chocolate chips
1 Cup dairy-free mini dark chocolate chips
1 Cup almonds, chopped

Directions:
Heat oven to 350. In a mixing bowl, combine margarine, sugar, and almond butter. Use an electric hand mixer and process until light and fluffy. Add the flax seeds, dairy-free milk, vanilla, water, corn starch, and coconut extract. Stir until all these ingredients are well combined. Set aside. In a separate bowl, combine the flour, cocoa, oatmeal, salt, baking soda, and baking powder. Mix until combined. Add the well-combined flour mix to the margarine mixture and stir. Add your coconut and dark chocolate chips and, once again, stir until combined. Bake for about 10 minutes,

depending on your preference for "doneness".
Remove the cookies from the oven and allow them to cool a minute, transfer to rack to cool completely.

Chocolate Cereal Bars
Ingredients
1 Cup Natural peanut butter
1/2 Cup agave nectar
1 Cup sugar
5 T. vegan margarine
6 Cups puffed rice cereal
1/2 Cup mini dairy-free chocolate chips

Directions
Grease a 9×13-inch pan and set aside. In a large saucepan, add peanut butter, agave, sugar, and margarine. Stir over medium heat until earth balance is melted, and the sugar is dissolved. Remove from heat and stir in puffed rice cereal. Stir in chocolate chips. The chocolate chips will melt giving the bars a chocolate color. Spread mixture into greased pan and press firmly down. Chill in refrigerator and the cut into squares, or fun shapes using cool cookie cutters!

Sweet Cinnamon Sticky Buns
Ingredients
For Dough:
2 Cups whole wheat flour
1 tsp Salt
1 tsp Baking Powder
4 tsp Vegan Butter
3/4 Cup Almond Milk

For Sprinkling:
2 tsp melted Vegan Butter
3/4 Cup Sugar
1 tsp cinnamon

Directions
Preheat oven to 450F. In a large bowl, combine flour, salt, and baking powder. Cut in the butter, then using your fingers massage the butter into the flour mixture. Pour the Milk into the flour/butter mixture until the dough gets thick and soft. Work the dough with your hands if necessary. Ball up the dough and set it out on a floured surface. Roll the dough into a long rectangular shape. Brush the top with melted butter and sprinkle with sugar/cinnamon mixture. Roll up and cut into slices. Place on a greased cookie sheet and bake until golden brown.

Monkey's Chocolate Chip Donuts

Ingredients
2 Cups white whole wheat flour *gluten free-substitute All-purpose gluten-free or Gluten-free rolled oat flour
1/3 Cup maple syrup or coconut sugar
1/4 Cup coconut oil
1 Cup unsweetened applesauce
1 mashed banana
2 T. almond or rice milk
1 tsp ground vanilla bean or extract
1 tsp cinnamon
1 tsp baking soda
1 tsp sea salt
1/4 Cup chocolate chips or carob chips

Directions
Preheat oven to 350 degrees. Mix all your dry ingredients in a large bowl. Mix wet into a second bowl. Add dry ingredients to the wet. Fold in carob or chocolate chips. Spoon batter into a greased donut pan. Bake for about 10-12 minutes or until your toothpick comes out clean.

Carrot Cake Balls
Ingredients
1 Large carrots, peeled
1 large apple, cored
1/8 Cup raisins or currants
1/2 Cup shredded coconut
1/4 tsp cinnamon
1/8 tsp or just a pinch of nutmeg
1-2 T. maple syrup, palm nectar or RAW honey
2 T. RAW nut butter- you choose kind
Raw cacao nibs for decoration
1/4 Cup coconut oil
2 T. raw honey
1/2 tsp vanilla
7 T. raw cacao-1TBSP extra for drizzling

Directions:
Grate the carrot and apple. Then press out as much juice as you can, by using a fine strainer. Add the rest of the ingredients, except the cacao nibs or toppings to the carrot/apple pulp. Mix well. Roll the dough into one-inch diameter balls. Chill the cake balls in your freezer. While the cake balls are chilling, you can prepare the chocolate. Start with room temperature coconut oil. In a mixing bowl, combine the melted coconut oil, pure vanilla extract, raw honey, and cocoa. Whisk together until the chocolate is smooth. Using a large fork, dip the cake balls into the chocolate. Let some of the chocolate drip off, then allow the chocolate to harden while you hold the stick. Then, sprinkle with a few cocoa nibs or nuts on top before it sets. Drizzle chocolate lines.

Pumpkin Spice Dip
Ingredients
1/2 Cup golden raisins
8 pitted and coarsely chopped Medjool dates
1/4 Cup almond milk
1 1/2 peeled and chopped organic apples, peeled, and chopped
1 can pumpkin purée
2 T. almond butter
2 tsp pumpkin pie spice
1 tsp organic apple cider vinegar
8 organic apples for dipping

Directions:
Put raisins in a small microwave-safe bowl and add water until barely covered. Microwave for one minute until raisins have plumped. Drain the water. Process chopped dates, raisins and 1/4 cup of almond milk in food processor or blender on highest setting, pulsing, and stopping to scrape as you go. Add peeled and cut apple; blend until mixture resembles fine chutney, pulsing. Add pumpkin puree, pumpkin pie spice, almond butter, and apple cider vinegar; blend at least 2-3 minutes or until smooth, pulsing and scraping occasionally. Transfer dip to serving cups or bowl. Slice your apples, other dip-in fruit, or ready the dipping cookies, crackers, etc.

Dig in, or dip in, on this occasion.

Chocolate Orange Avocado Pudding
Ingredients
2 small organic avocados
1/3 Cup organic orange juice
4 T. cocoa
3 T. agave or raw honey

Directions:
Remove the skin and pit your avocados. Next, place avocados in a food processor or blender with cocoa, honey and 1/4 cup of freshly squeezed organic orange Blend for a few minutes, until the pudding is thick. Remove the lid and scrape the sides to ensure it is combined well. If the pudding is too thick, add a splash of orange juice. Replace the lid and blend again for a few seconds if necessary.

Taste and add more sweetener and cocoa if need be. Place pudding in a resealable bowl or cover with plastic wrap. Place in the fridge to set. Serve cold.

Chocolate Mousse

Ingredients
1 can coconut milk
1/3 Cup cocoa powder
1 Cup packed dried dates
Just a few drops of vanilla extract

Directions:
Pit your dates and blend well with coconut milk using a hand mixer. Add, the cocoa powder, with a few drops of pure vanilla extract and blend well. Divvy into serving cups and refrigerate until set.
Indulge in your healthy, fluffy, chocolatey snack!

Vegan Lemon Meltaways
Ingredients
1 Cup cashew flour
1 Cup raw coconut flour
1/4 tsp salt
2 T. maple syrup
3 lemons
1 1/2 tsp vanilla extract
1/3 Cup coconut oil

Directions:
Put all ingredients into a food processor and process until well combined. Take out about one spoonful at a time and roll them in the palms of your hands to form a spherical shape. Leave plain or roll in shredded coconut flakes, crushed nuts, broken peppermint candy, M&M type candy, almond flour, or powdered sugar. Put them in the refrigerator to firm for about 20 minutes. Keep them refrigerated until ready to serve. Enjoy cool!

Vegan Twinkie Cake
Ingredients
2 T. chia seeds
1/4 Cup and 1 T. water
1/4 Cup vegan butter
1 T. coconut spread
1/3 Cup organic maple syrup
1 tsp pure vanilla extract
3/4 Cup Almond flour
1/4 tsp baking soda

Directions:
Combine chia and water, sit at room temperature to gel. Cream the vegan butter, coconut spread, vanilla, and maple syrup. Add chia and combine more completely. Add almond flour and baking soda to mixture. Keep blending. Divide the batter between three mini bread loaf pans. Bake at 350 degrees F for 25 minutes. Cool completely.

Vanilla Cake
Ingredients
1 1/2 Cup almond flour + 3 T. all-purpose certified gluten-free flour
1 Cup white sugar
1 tsp baking soda
1/2 tsp fine sea salt
1 tsp white vinegar
1 1/2 tsp vanilla extract
5 T. organic coconut oil
1 Cup water

Directions
Preheat oven to 350 degrees F. Mix dry ingredients- both flours, sugar, baking soda and salt. In an oiled 8-inch baking pan. Make 3 depressions in dry ingredients - two small dents, one larger. Pour white vinegar in one depression, vanilla in the second and coconut oil in third larger dip. Pour water over all. Mix until smooth. Bake in preheated oven for 30 minutes. Check with toothpick to determine that cake is done. Cool on rack. Top with your favorite frosting.

Sugar and Cinnamon Chips

Ingredients
Flour tortillas
Melted butter or Extra virgin olive oil
Cinnamon
Sugar

Directions:
Line baking sheet with parchment paper. Preheat your oven to 350 degrees F. Combine sugar and ground cinnamon in a large bowl. Stack your flour tortillas, and cut into 1/8ths, small triangular pieces. Place the triangles on the baking sheet, brush lightly with extra virgin olive oil or melted butter, flip over and brush second sides too. Place in center of oven and bake until crisp. Remove from oven and lightly brush with more melted butter. Gently toss the baked and oiled chips in the cinnamon sugar, careful as the chips may be hot. Serve at room temperature.

Vegan Jell-O
Ingredients:
1 tablespoon Agar Agar powder
2 Cups organic, no sugar added juice
A little maple syrup or agave to taste

Directions
Put the agar agar and juice and sweetener in a medium saucepan, whisk together. Bring to a boil over low-medium heat, stirring consistently. Reduce to the lowest heat setting and simmer five minutes. Remove from heat, pour in to cups. This will set at room temperature or in the refrigerator in about 30 minutes.

Spiced Almond Milk
Ingredients
2 Cups almond milk
1 T. all natural, organic maple syrup
1/4 tsp nutmeg
1/8 tsp cinnamon

Directions:
Place all ingredients in a blender. Blend until will incorporated, about one minute

Enjoy!

Vegan Orange Julius
Ingredients
1 1/2 Cups almond milk
1/2 Cup orange juice concentrate
1 tsp pure vanilla extract
6 ice cubes

Directions:
Combine in blender. Mix approximately one minute and serve cold.

Vegan Banana Pops
Ingredients
Bananas
Silk or Whole soy yogurt
Crushed cookies, graham crackers, or granola of choice
more topping ideas: mini chocolate chips, cinnamon sugar mixture, chopped nuts, shredded coconut
wooden sticks for inserting in the bananas

Directions:
Add crushed cookies or granola into a pie plate. Peel your bananas and cut them in half. Then push a wooden stick into each half. Roll bananas in yogurt and press into crushed cookies or granola. Add in other toppings you'd like. Place on a wax paper lined cookie sheet and freeze until serving.

Vanilla Avocado Banana "Ice Cream"
Ingredients
1 ripe avocado
1 banana
1 tsp pure vanilla extract
1/2 Cup coconut milk
1/2 Cup sugar- stevia or agave can also be used
1 cup ice cubes

Directions:
Blend everything in blender until smooth. Store in the freezer. Mixture will freeze solid in the freezer and if so, let thaw for a few minutes on the counter, until you are able scoop easily.

Banana Bread Biscotti

Ingredients
1 Cup raw almonds
1 T. flax meal
1 ripe banana
3 Medjool dates, pitted
1 T. pure maple syrup
1/2 tsp baking soda
1/8 tsp fine sea salt
1/2 tsp pure vanilla extract
1 T. raw walnuts
1 T. vegan dark chocolate chips

Directions:
Preheat oven to 350F. Using a food processor, pulse the almonds into a fine flour. Add the flax meal, banana, dates, maple syrup, baking soda, salt, and vanilla extract to the food processor. Blend until a thick dough forms. Add the walnuts and chocolate chips. Pulse a couple of times to distribute throughout the dough. On a baking sheet lined with parchment paper or a Silpat baking mat, form the dough into a rectangular log about 6×4 inches.
Bake for 27 minutes, or until the top has browned. Cool until firm enough to transfer to a cooling rack (about 10 minutes). Transfer to the cooling rack and continue to cool until firm enough to slice (another 10 minutes). Slice crosswise into 8 biscotti slices. Preheat the oven to 350 degrees F. Return the cookies to the lined baking sheet. Bake for an additional 10 minutes. Cool to room temperature. Indulge!

Printed in Great Britain
by Amazon